TUNNELS IN THE SNOW

TUNNELS IN THE SNOW

Selected Poems by
ÁRPÁD FARKAS

Translated from the Hungarian by

PAUL SOHAR
(sohar.paul@gmail.com)

Published by Iniquity Press/Vendetta Books
in cooperation with
Concord Media Jelen (Irodalmi Jelen), Arad, Romania

Editor-in-Chief: Zoltán Böszörményi
Cover and book design: Farkas Király

Website: www.irodalmijelen.hu

Printing House: Ingram Content Group LLC

ISBN US: 978-1-877968-50-1
ISBN RO: 978-973-7927-37-8

CONTENTS:

PROLOGUE:
ÁRPÁD FARKAS AND HIS POETRY

This Transylvanian poet is at home everywhere: in the world, in his homeland, in the cataclysm of feelings and in the white heat of reasoning. He is characterized equally by the hardness of oaks and the tender nature of wild flowers. He hit the road, and like the hero of folktales, he has just about reached his goals. He speaks all fired up and with the conviction of the enthralled. He often raises an arm, never to hit someone, but to beckon or signal or pat; he is not infected by the violence of our time.

Formal and free verse do not simply alternate in his hands but almost associate in order to give immaculate expression to an experience. It would be hard to point out a contemporary poet who can use form in the service of meaning as successfully. Almost every one of his experiences creates its own form; his poetry is a series of successful birthing. All this testifies to inner order; even though our age does not lack in injured souls, overgrown by cancerous burdens and unable to free themselves. This poet is wholesome in the original sense of the word. He wants for nothing; he has found his place in the world; he unblinkingly faces the problems of our time and his personality—he can work out the dramatic harmony of our era.

A significant part of contemporary poetry is infested with a new linguistic fungus: vaguely conceived sentences. Árpád Farkas is known for the sincerity, clarity and bravery of his declarative sentences. He can speak openly because his soul and sensation of life are open, which ensures that he never for a minute falls behind the turmoil of the world. As a result, he does not lack in judgment and can evaluate human events; he can jubilate as well as protest. The poets of old also served as watchmen, bells alerting the community, prophets with foresight, medicine men who had balm for every wound. This kind of calling is burning inside Árpád Farkas.

Géza Féja
(Writer, journalist)

UPON OUR FATHERS' FACES

(Apáink arcán)

Here in Erdély, mudslides flow
deep inside the men at dark;
with a crackle the cheekbones grow,
and the shadows in the gullies mark

with millennial stare which forest is
burning on the shores of restraint.
The grassy fields were smeared with slogans
and the blood of calves in vain;

the men's unruly manes ignite a song,
forest-fire-like they roam,
their handsome rebel faces phosphoresce,
showing us the way back home.
My lads,
    my lads, you prancing colts in wild winds,
should we fail to leap beyond the stars ahead
and descend back on our craggy land,
let's go softly, on tiptoes!:
it's on our fathers' faces that we tread.

(Erdély is the Hungarian name for Transylvania; pronounced air-day-y.)

AT THE AGE OF TWENTY

(Húszévesen)

I join your circle with my jacket tossed
casually over my shoulders: you may draw
your fingers on my slender ribs
and cut open the hot and naked song—

I've outgrown the red-eared
wonders of puberty; what I dreamed
two years ago now scratches my shoulders,
offers me my father's desires;
I wear out his shirts—

My fires are purified: even in a downpour
I burn, I have a love;
it has almost made me a man,
and with it
I would not cheat
on this manhood: I stay pure,
like a kiss in the rain—

This Age has outgrown
the wide-eyed wonders of puberty;
in my squinting eyes the flames
are piercing: to live at the age of twenty
fully responsible for these Twenty Years—
anyone aflame like this, even if with
silvery hair, is my contemporary—

I join your circle with my jacket
tossed casually over my shoulders:
draw your fingers on my slender
ribs; I no longer ask
if my song is wanted or not;
I do not button up!

MY MOTHER

(Anyám)

Stay, she begged me but I had to hit the road.
She packed a piece of sky, deep within me stowed.
I spread it out and in it, wherever I trod,
I formed a planet from a pinch of homeland sod.
I settled it with scenery and crowded bazaars
and covered it with foal-faced thirsty-staring stars;
my nights were blessed with new hopes and fabulous
schemes,
but sometimes they would drain my blood in exchange
for dreams.
At last, I turned back home, my planet squeaking of my
pride;
rolling it, I rambled it for my mom inside
the kitchen where the light was good...
Her greetings to her son were:
"Go out, my dear, and get a load of kindling wood."

LET THERE BE NO SILENCE

(Csak csend ne legyen)

Let wispy little voices spring from blocks
of dumbstruck dawns, let them flood the borders
of glistening fields, let them ring out on
the plates of daisies in a buzzing sunrise;
let linden trees, the xylophones of toning roads,
speak up when morning wipes
her rosy finger on their leaves.

Whether the cranked or the pole kind,
let wells squeak; let buckets nod
to the splashing call of depths:
let crock pots, chips and nicks,
let them be rattling wings
slinging me high
over my dreams!

Let wimpy whetstones roar on the edges of scythes,
and you, too, stocky anvils under hammer blows

...my people, oh grant me a wish, my dream,
And give me a true thrashing machine,
with the blanket license
to buzz and howl to me!
but let there be no silence!
but let there be no silence!

The price of silence is silence by rule,
like yellow mould under haystacks; a tool
of zigzagging thoughts, thin and bland
like a wagon trail in driven sand.

Let all those who live here live like this:
holding on to the wind with leafy neuron hiss,
let them not wallow in lazy rest
of woolly sheep in rocking nest.

Let them be happy with magnificent pain
and keep their dreams on iron bread,

and not wait for the splotches of death
to bloom on their deep blue dread.

This's how I live. I wake the dawn winds,
disperse the red lady bugs of the stray
stars and send sound on its
peculiar, long, rumbling way.
I want wild, enthralling cataracts!
Let the rattling rhythms of labor batter me,
let them hold my shapeless reverie
in their shapely hands.

HANGOVER SONG

(Másnapos ének)

A spectral, slow wind starts to roll now
from the dungeons of the dawn, the late blue flames
of alcohol are losing heart.
The seven dwarves sit only at the depths of daybreak
clutching now the frozen bones of horror,
and through the pores of our skin
a gooey glow breaks out:
nausea's flowers overrun our faces.

How much startled anxiety can a poor soul dredge up
on the morning after,
when the mist creeps through his clammy shirt
and festers between his fetid fingers as he reaches up
into the gluey sky for the birds
floundering up there.

The chic shirt doesn't count now,
neither does the peek-a-boo smile
of the cuff links...
Like a lost wet dog, his fur licked down by rain,
he slinks through the stale wakening
of the cities,
and in his eyes the rancid question begs:
    "did I maul you badly?
        did I kill you? did I?"
and he's convinced that
his corrosive breath ruffles the rose
petals in the roadside dew.

How many frozen tigers, ready to leap,
may be slumbering inside us...
How many sins may be swirling in the deep,
if the cooling-off hours of delirium
stare at them with so much trepidation!...

...Well now, let the final answers grow
from the sober work of our daylight
and the mild-mannered circles of our fingerprints
as they swim slowly out of our view.

TEENAGER ROMANCE

(Kamasz szerelem)

I caught a glimpse of you.

The noise split open like the smooth skin
of an overripe plum,
and on a silent clue
the yellow Sun
plopped down to Earth's colorful din.

This mood banged inside me, and I fell in love with you.

Since then, always and every place,

wherever earth smells of freshly baked bread
I take you,

I swirl you around, ˙

I display you
to the next lover ahead.

LOVE, YOUNG PONY

(Szerelem, kiscsikó)

Let's tie a bell to its neck, a small bell to its neck;
let it go galloping inside us—
our pastures are big and wide.

I shall never keep it on a rope, not on a rope;
in my hand no grass grows for it—
I catch lightning bolts in bone-breaking wind.

And if at times I get driven off, driven very far
from you by a rainstorm, I listen with
bated breath and a silencing finger held high:
can we still hear it ring
in our pastures' green deepening?

WARM WIND

(Meleg szél)

Strangely purplish was the sky,
when the scared kid crossed the valley
in his string-handled pot fresh, frothing milk snorted,
the fields sensuously panted all around,
steaming hills were mating with animal sounds,
branches were giggling, the roadside
mulberry trees tittering lecherously—
the kid kept going, stealing his way,
and the bottom of his feet were burning like his skin,
the little creek too was giggling,
oh, no, not under the willow,
but here, on the periphery of the nose—
he took a lick; my god, it's salty!

THE ELEGY OF NAGYSZOROS

(Nagyszoros elégiája)

The throat of my village, oh, Nagyszoros,
I was the prince with the wooden sword inside you,
a giggle bubbling up to heaven, the little son of crying,
and the heart of my teeny-tiny village beating in its throat;
the tickling vegetable fragrance of suppers, the carefree
need as it spread its patience over
the handful of sky, the gardens, the porches.
Nagyszoros, oh, Nagyszoros, from inside you my great-grand-
                                  fathers
tore themselves out at blood-red dawns, those busy ants,
you swallowed, you vomited wagons loaded with manure,
with their wheels shackled and with gung-ho cracking of whips
they bled into the open,
cussing palled into prayer until, through you from the depths,
it reached the light—

The throat of my village, oh, Nagyszoros,
I was the prince with the wooden sword once inside you,
the one who climbs up on the vines and duels with the thistles
and swings from the maples
or from stray straws anywhere,
your Adam's apple danced under my bare feet to the beat of
                                  church
bells: a shadow of the steeple-top—
your games turned me wild, you clawed my nails sharp,
you tickled me into a little lad,
and then love came to call for me, yes it did,
in the image of Zsuzsanna—

Indeed she came, Zsuzsanna, the wee fair beauty among the
                                  beauties
of Szoros, between her toes the mud was squirting,
her sky-purplish skin glistened from blackberries,
she trudged behind the wagon, picking her nose,
coming closer and closer, as if out of a fairytale,
her cute little ankles were washed by the foam of
horse urine flooding the ruts in the road,

there she came, skipping over crusty cow dung,
with a stray straw in her golden locks,
she suddenly turned into a queen
   just so that a king I might become—

Zsuzsanna's hair then did not yet have color,
lips she didn't have, her eyes did not look like anything.
With tiny beads and mud balls my darling pelted me,
I grabbed her thick hair, her tears welled up, and I got scared,
promised her little birds, with golden feathers,
I led her into a hollow covered with tall grass,
to titter and giggle among the mint and heather.
Hollering farmers drove by in their whipping wagons,
and look: whispers were crawling under the shrubs
—we glistened at each other with the glow of
fireflies like those who have no inkling of the secret yet they
fear it already. When the coast was clear she bounced up
ready to flee, but I—who knows why?—
begged her: let's play: it might start raining!
And to protect her I lay down on her tummy. I started to stir
with the movements of mating stallions and bulls I'd seen,
and her pretty eyes widened into questioning circles,
her butterfly breath flitted against the frightened ferns—
my god, what gasps! How could I suspect that
that voice would grow up, transfigured
like baby whimper into sobs?!......

...And peace into silence the wheezing draft stirs up
sweeping with it life and dreams up to heaven—and myself
to this globescape—, and the throat of my tiny village,
clogged up by ruins ,
can swallow no more——
At the edge of Nagyszoros the drowning life still
sends out an afterglow and, just for a flag, Zsuzsanna's teeny
plaid skirt, the holy banner
of our one-time purity
      keeps flapping-slapping up here————

NOON

(Dél)

You roll in the crackly-dry grass—that's it.
The sky drizzles on your face;
your breath slightly billows its
corner, and you feel how weightless it is.
Near your head a wild dill plant opens its parachute;
Earth puts its arms around you,
and now it's floating,
no longer in a dive.

GIRLS ON THE FARM

(Lányok a tanyán)

Lunar barking of dogs, snow: white whispering
    cascades, sprints off, swirls on the farm.
          Oh, you girls,
       need has put you up here
        like jam for winter,
       preservative-snow
    drizzles on your skin and snuggles,
        lying low.

You, my unsullied ones, you—aren't the nights tough?
The bearers of first love arrive, one by one they come,
    each happens to stop by—
he scrapes on the threshold, scratches on the latch,
    and—crack!—the fence plank
       swings in the wind...

All that's needed is a caress,
   a dream to sew on
or a shirt button
    at the least...

SEPTEMBER

(Szeptember)

A heavy drinker is too shy to holler, lips glued to the glass,
like mine are to summer, I'll never let it pass!
Drunken autumn depresses me, makes me thirsty and
                                        cold,
    like the drinking gypsy wearies
    the violin
    clenched
    under his chin.

STORY

(Történet)

At exactly two-forty-five
by Central European Time, light appeared on the horizon;
snow brought blinding whiteness
and nine larks.
They broke into a song inspired by the unexpected
shiny organ pipes of the freeze under the eaves,
and the carefully placed masks on the night table
melted,
guest hair started to grow,
the artificial bones of prostheses clicked.
Sleepy humanity sat up in bed, dropping
the covers with meat-red bald face
and, modestly holding a hand out front,
made a beeline toward the restroom, to the Moon.

No matter. For a minute everything became clear.
The lifeless remains of the nine larks were of no help
in the snow above the Tropic of Capricorn.

BELLS

(Harangok)

Because it's been a long time since firestorms and floods
had devastated this city
and danger seemed far away,
the bell towers fell into benign neglect—,
till one morning all of them collapsed into dust.

Since then, broken loose, brown bells have been
clunking in the voluminous air,

and no one can hear them— —

CROSSING THE BORDER

(Határátkelés)

The train is running with me on the sly,
and my mother's home-baked bread
is rolling with the full moon of Erdély,
rounded to the shade of wine, deep red;
my father scatters fire sparks
behind us; he's sharpening
my pencil with his fishing knife:
let's have light on everything!

My hyacinth-eyed little girl
is swinging on the moon's nice curl,
her pure-white weeping handkerchief
is my woman's to wave and kiss.
The train is running; on the shore
of potato fields, dancing little deer,
bushes, hills, pine-forested land,
red-dotted puffy cheeks appear
slurping milk with puffs and sighs,
two million faces bear these lines,
the prey of fate—and a heavy load
come with me in my pocket stowed
with loose tobacco powder trash,
my motherland—my total cache
and burden—that's what I take away;
well, you customs men, tell me,
what's the duty I have to pay?

THE WALLED-UP PULPIT IN VIENNA

(A befalazott szószék)

Solid citizens still hang out in the plaza in front
of Stephansdom, sitting before the walled-up pulpit
of Saint John of Capestrano; they've been sitting here
for centuries in the steaming warm piss of carriage horses;
around them the bombs of spread-out animal legs explode,
but they keep munching on Wiener schnitzel without batting
                                            an eye;
this is where cherubim gather on the bones; next block the
                                            classier
folks of the Graben wag the flag of riches:—the magic carpet!
Kapisztrán János sometimes emerges from the sacristy with
a pitcher of Burgenländer red
—they imbibe! Skat cards keep flipping!
Hey, you restless soul,
what good would it do here if we started
clanging the indifferent bells
of this indifferent
European continent?

Saint John de Capestrano, 1366-1456, was an Italian priest who rallied the Hungarian troops under Hunyadi János to defend Belgrade against the invading Ottoman Turks; thus, he is known in Hungary as Kapisztrán János.

ABROAD

I'm hanging out here under Europe's bright-lit windows
with the moonlight's heavenly lime dripping from my
face,
clawed red by the wind, enwrapped by a shower:
    the waters of the Danube and Olt pour
    and wash the tatters of my mantle.

Driven by hunger, your sole son has strayed far from the
herd
        and staggers in your winds, oh liberty!
        Through the veils of rain
        he feels the century's blind face,
    with mud-caked boots he keeps on kicking
    Mozart's cradle:—let him bawl!

    I bump into everything!
    All I want is just to walk on nicely, whistling in the
rain,
    (the china houses weep when I splatter mud on
them),
and whispering sweet nothings to the foliage in secret
    (while knocking the castle off the hill
    with my clumsy elbow! The statue of the ETERNAL
SONGSTER
    turns to dust when I try a tune!).

My rain-soaked, homesick shadow is cast
    only to the moon from here,
    oh, Twentieth Century!

Though at home how peaceful and how open the herd is
now,
steaming and fattening, pressed against the planks!
At the end of the first millennium of the great migrations
I cannot picture a better home
        than there,
    where even the brother bites your back,

not only the friend,
where the people chump on the flowers of barbarian
pastures,
warm up by their stench,
and bare their knuckles for mere morsels of civilization!

I'm hanging out here under Europe's open windows,
a sudden wild squall blows the moonlight off my face,
all the way back home.

THE SEVEN DWARVES

(A hét törpe)

Tossed together
knives and flowers found;
I journey into autumn,
I journey winter-bound.
Half-dead by dreams
my unguarded soul
feels like sharp knives;
I call it a flower pole.

I build it from nothing,
trust it with verve—
seven dwarves dancing
on many a nerve,
tacking together my smile,
my tantrums on a tarp;
in my heart seven little
axes set off a spark.

So what if it shows:
the song isn't rap,
in the white of Snow
White's teeth a gap...
With smarting eyes I wish
I didn't have to see
my treasures tossed
in a ditch with me.

My laboring lungs
doing better and more,
a bird in flight
with a drumming score,
flowers using knives,
knives with flower sound...
I journey into autumn,
I journey winter-bound.

SHARP RAIN

(Éles eső)

Sharp rain, tasting of iron, is coming down;
your face gets entangled with its metallic lines:—
you may glow with wet moss and snails
if you can stand it till morning shine.

My face is different: much scarier.
Merciless cold spells have settled on it
in thin, bluestone-layered sediments;
the traces of a kiss dissolve, caresses peel off,
a horrible rattle bends
across the temples.

Maybe that's the price of purity.
Razor rain is coming down; I let it fall.
Love deposits as nitrate salt upon my brow,
making it collapse like a rain-seared wall.

DOORS AND WINDOWS

(Ajtók és ablakok)

Where I'm come from, you doors
and lightning-lit window panes,
you showered me with light
and the wings of magic planes;

and yet you had no house of your own,
you were built in empty skies
with the view of wild flights,
your door- and window-eyes;

four walls were attracted and built
by the swoosh of angel wings,
I've never crawled into a house under
a threshold in all my wanderings;

while I blindly braved the dark
I received from your glow
a chink of the blue sky at night,
that was all you had to show.

With broken wings I stand ready,
now while it's still allowed—,
but you, let yourselves stay afloat!,
and keep floating like a cloud!

THE LAUGHING YOU

(Nevetésed)

Those tiny silver bells, who stole them into you?
That warm little breeze, when is it born
and how long can it flit about beneath your ribs,
brushing there against the silver bells singing?

Rivers, too, are babbling deep inside you.
Emerald woods and mountains beckon through your
eyes.
But what light has blessed the fields
whence those white daisies of your peals
of laughter pour out, tumbling toward me?

At times like these I'm but a little kid in shorts,
hopping around on one leg,
punching into the soft belly of the air
and chasing clickety-click steel hoops
or ringing the bell on my bike
to scare apart the lovers in the park.

Let them gather, all inside the porcelain sheen
glorifying domes of joy;
let them all imbibe the warbles
bubbling up from crystal depths unseen.
Let them all feel the ringing of wheat sheaves,
the wakening of mountains
and the whirlpools of forests
when you burst out laughing
and green waterfalls
leap out of your voice.

Keep on pouring, you flood of sweetness;
wash the salt out of my skin,
the dark shadows from under my eyes
and dissolve the spasms of daily toil
in me where only your laughter heals.

To my dying day my purity
will preserve your ringing peals.

CARESSES

(Simogatás)

When the words inside us are in cinders
what keeps on shining,
                purring,
                        and caressing
is the hand.

In its quiet streams resides a calm.
It opens up my fingers—
                the petals of my palm,
and while by this flower
                your cheeks are gently fanned—
they pick up the mood and temper of my hand.

Everything I've ever touched
        burns below my skin,
every cheek I've ever stroked
        touches now your chin,
and since on some cheeks this hand's had a painful ride,
—now it feels your face to see itself inside.

When the words inside us have all but burnt away
let yourself inhale and soak in
        the shining,
            the purring
                the caressing
of the hand.

OUR HEART'S IDEAL LOVE

(Szívünk szép szerelme)

Summer was still broiling in Esztelnek town,
when I heard my major domo lovey-dove:
eat and drink, before this heat spell
cools the mind and our heart's ideal love.

And I stuffed myself. Slices of the hill nearby,
the innards of love and its peels pulled off
were roasted on a fire, and the tongues of flames
whispered: she'd be my heart's ideal love.

I'd seen many a man and woman get lost
in the delirium of passing affairs of love;
even if she crosses her creek without a blush,
she'd surely be my heart's ideal love.

She surely had a shirt in her chest
big enough to hold two hearts;
in shirt-ripping, unruly, feverish unrest
we'd be throbbing together enough
to rip garments and vestments off of us,
exposing our heart's ideal love.

DANCE

(Tánc)

In August's quiet clearings
    where the two of them were wed,
a birch and a beech start dancing
    by a coolish airstream led.

In her arms the blue swirl swings
    and love's merry soft-green sparks
shimmer slyly through the chinks
    in the lisping leaves and barks.

In this swing we must believe
    while the muted ball can last,
beyond the dance, beyond the trees,
    summer's breeze boils off so fast.

THE SMOKE OF SUMMERS

(Nyarak füstje)

Smoldering in deep summers, the dead
keep spinning in cast iron quietude,
the gleam of their bones is a phosphorescent
skirt wound around me, sparkling but mute;
I've become the axle of this severe
summer and its phony brightness here.

Slowly mumbling to myself I ask
you folks to stop laughing at this jerk
just because around him amass
the slaughtered and the uninterred.

First in line is pop, the peasant saint,
the sons bring his nine-acre tract
he'd hidden under splintered fingernails,
for which lean summers had him whacked.

Next is uncle, the flunky, paid with a bullet,
now he's like a nail from a rotting board,
his chalk-white bone falls into silence
from dampish death consumed by mold.

Another comes from far infinity.
Blood is seeping from his mouth, a song.
He still looks somewhat half-demented,
though his flames are only candle-strong.

***

And they come beribboned;
the depths of night-dark eye sockets
send up smoke to rise,
swirling over my heart.
The fingers of the living swish,
crackling golden swagger stick,
they ripped you once apart,
now digging into one another's flesh

they brawl for feed, for what's due,
because that's what they do
for the smoke, the smoke that swirls and whirls
from golden smoke rings, skull-dwelling pearls!
Greed again likes to poke
at the tinsel veil of smoke;
oh, you of hexed meat, you the smoke
of burned beliefs, go and fly high,
go shaking through our hearts;
provide new faith for the struggle,
don't let punk dare-devils rinse
their faces in your inner bins;
rocket into the lily screams
of the flower pyre reams,
tremble on a tulip
my violet, my only treasure hoard,
my upright spinal cord,
only you can save me now!

(Prophecy)

One day the smoke will rise,
the glittering diamond will lie
in the place of honor, the ground,
under a hematoma sky.

THE ABLUTIONS OF OLD MEN

(Mikor az öregemberek mosakodnak)

centuries-old rain pours from the shriveled-up palms of their hands, glistens in the gullies of their faces, that's how they wash up, the old men, with their legs spread, with john-the-baptist dignity bending over the glazed-tin wash bowl, that's how they wash up, as if it were for the last time they were washing up, they don't bother wrapping a towel around their waists, the water sprays on the trousers, it doesn't matter, the measured and deliberate lathering-rubbing movement works over the entire skin surface, harasses the pores: with leisurely, pensive and stretching movements wash up the old men, from their minute gasps the water is atomized, and from behind the curtain of falling rinse water the images of their bending so often over a three-quarters of a century emerge, bending to pick up a stick from the ground, to scoop up some drink water from a brook, that's how they bent over the brook standing on the shores of Irtysh or Tisza, with the bayoneted rifles leaning against a bush, when stumbling bent over in a headlong chase of the enemy or else on the run away from it, scorching the earth, and sniffing it as they wiped off the blood; that's how they wash up, the old men, as if they were washing off the dirt of a three-quarters of a century, like those who would have always liked to live cleanly, in a freshly toweled mood; nowadays it's only on Sunday mornings that the old men wash up like this, only before funerals when they have to see off an old cohort who's never to return, that's how they wash up, that's right, exactly, the old men, as if they were washing up for the last time, as if they wanted to enter with unsullied glow into the source of all that pristine wheat, into the old sod of the motherland that their bodies will enrich turning to dust.

When old men are washing up it's the Twentieth Century that's bending over emerald waters with a huge hunger for cleansing.

OLD FOLKS

(A vének)

They're sitting in the opalescent weather
under the eaves; it's snowing, coming
down in enormous Central-Asian flakes.

Lambs are coming down or rabbits,
neighing milk-white stallions—:
with them winter plays fairy tales.

A crayon sketch emerges from behind
the rough curtain of snowfall—:
King Dul's naked daughters dance.

The old folks get up with arms stretched,
and hesitantly, like the blind, they merge
with the shower of the shining light.

MIGRANT WORKERS

(Lipovánok)

They dig. They migrate from barracks to barracks
as ballast for this wobbly Earth.
From the Milky Way they brought the wheelbarrow.
To another planet they might be carting dirt.
On their skin the salty smells of oceans foam,
in their hands the shovels faintly whimper:
—can we ever turn back home?

None but a small nation's son digs as if below the skin
and shovels dirt as if deep from within.
And the pickax he swings high
as if its job were to destroy
a chain link of an old alloy,
the weight of built-up solid ice
on the mind and on the nerve,
on remembrance, secret yet precise.

None but a small nation's son has to meet the world
from behind the bars of his ten fingers;
he doesn't stuff himself when hungry, doesn't eat—
nourishment is what he takes!
The bottom of the emptied herring can
gleams to him of endless ocean wakes.

Indestructible is the one who endures the sea,
he can but give even as his body's giving up,
he guards the universe instead of conquering it,
even the Milky Way turns to him for milk with a cup.

He's the one about to pass out in the blasts of wind,
but still hangs in there—at whatever cost,
he who earns the awe of winter, summer, fall,
and their wonder without ever getting lost,

he's the one who's able, buried waist deep in dirt,
to keep on giving with a grin,
and to stare with blessing eyes back at the world.
Exiles, every one of you my kin!

THE GREENING PLOW HANDLES

(Kizöldült ekeszarvak)

That morning the garden eagles turned green...
and the plow handles burst out with green leaves.

The earth shook itself
and the century-old pearls
of human perspiration
rolled down ringing on plowshares—

A woman took a handful of them home,
and used them to glue up a crack in the oven.

SIGNAL

(Jel)

Wind is whipping the woods,
its bone-trees are alight.

They all have scrambled out,
suspiciously walk around,
all creatures alive now fight.

This is what fall is. Devouring, wild!
Still chewing on bones…

I hear the soft crack
of fingers knuckling

on my throat.

And squinting, like someone
stretching a bow

—clenching teeth on teeth— ,
with my fingers curled I peel

his fingers off my throat,

and tensed up blue, I shake;

I entreat you, my beasts: use this break
to flee now, and on the run!

Make your escape!

I REMAIN

(Maradok)

The prodigal I am, the son the landscape
picks up pressing me against its chest,
my nostrils are invaded by the thorns of weeds
and the arm-pit smell of rotting hay,
its bristly, rough face scrapes my face
while its sharp cheek is in my gullet,
in its fingers my back bones crunch and crumple,
my strength is darting between my scalp and soles.

Wait a minute! Stop loving me, just for a minute!

Out of its bold stranglehold of patience
I'd flood the fields and sky with goose bumps,
whisper bed sheets to snuggle underneath the woods,
herd all the creeks into the ocean,
or fall in with a flock of wild flowers.

There's a penchant for gushing
and for generous love dawning within me
along with so much sober attachment
that, throbbing though my temples are,
I still wait
and remain—

THE PLASTER ELF OF OUR GARDEN

(Kerti törpe)

The plaster elf is on the watch,
eavesdropping on every sound.
His report now should be ready
to banish anyone around.

You installed the plaster elf
to watch the roses of the yard,
he was supposed to stay out there
as the roses' faithful guard.

Watching our house is the elf
strolling up and down the grass.
If he winks the house is circled
by his wretched ilk en masse.

FLUTE SONG

(Furulyaszó)

When the evening sinks into the quake of ferns
the silence of the glaciers is rent
by the singing of a flute.
It slides under the landscape on dewdrop ball bearings
while in the heavens of manger-sized hamlets
bays a lamb and neighs a brute.

They graze on the smoke of measly little suppers,
messing up the dreams
of kind church-social folks.
Only apple blossom rings out
from sun-forsaken backyards,
and has its fragile gleam
blown to distant cities
by the singing of the flute.

Now it's only this tune, this pentatonic song,
that keeps us well. Brings us close, cheek to cheek.
With its blinking dawns the land guards
its blossom-fragile
treasure trove.

THE SILENCE OF MOTHERS

(Anyák némasága)

Only children stare at knives with avid horror.
A loaf of bread sings like a violin when squeezed
against the breasts of mothers who slice it;
the lightning gleam winked by the knife is snow-soft music.
Children turn their faces to the morsels' snowfall;
it's only they who stare with avid horror
at the knife-blade racing towards their mothers.

The mothers soon depart from us, like empty vessels
vacated by our dreams;
like the glasses, mugs and spoons back home, their breasts
preserve the cold shape of our lips.

The wind forges us into men; the grinding-stone of time
hones us into knives.

Only mothers stare with avid, voiceless horror
at their sons,
as they race like bread-knives to their mothers' breasts.

WHEN YOU COME

(Ha majd jössz)

I'll spread out the train whistles before you,
the sounds of waiting fluttering in me,
I'll spread before you the scent
of breakfast omelets fleeting
through an open window
when you come.

And my cloud-hopping dreams will bow to the ground.

They will kneel down somewhere under
the pear trees of the yard and snicker
at the awkwardness of that first kiss
that I had kneaded and smoothed out
on the corner of my pillow on lonely, hairy nights.

And the milk bottles huddling on the doorstep
will get out of your way,
the white brides of daybreaks
will stand back when you come.

We'll roam among the currant bushes of the garden,
and I'll tell you all about the big joys of small towns.

EYELASH FOREST

(Szempillaerdő)

I come to your clearings to rest,
I sleep there, a tired prince
escaping all enemies,
while your deer are licking my brow
your birds land on my shoulders,
your beasts make friends with me;
let all blessings come to this sheltering,
tiny joy,
and let it not cast a shadow on me,

                    *

let your eyelash forest whisper, breathe
above me, and caress me
to new awakenings, new fights.
.

FORCEFUL GAME

(Makacs játék)

Like a sleeping pineapple bud,
this love exploded with fair might....
We're its petals sent now flying far,
the wind holds us together tight.

We could fly into outer space,
but the city doesn't let us flee—
A forceful game thunders through
our blood, yet letting us go free—

The pathway-strings of the fields
are strumming a great new song,
while we fly off tweeting like a pair
of eighth notes with flags as long.

And then the day comes to a halt,
and so does the afternoon...
there can be no sunset where
the two of us intone our tune.

AT THE TRAIN STATION

(Egy állomáson)

Age will make me grumpy, too depraved to die,
a roguish old fart, whistling with a fag
stuck between my lips when I see you
in the station ticket-booth as a stern old bag

who, peering with disdain above her specs,
tilts her head to take a better look at me.
The engines' laughter will then split the night:
"Redeemed is what the old rogue wants to be!"

And the old rogue will then watch the flowers burst
into bloom and stallions kick up aging feet
inside him, but then, with chin tucked in
pickpocket-style, he'll slink back to the street,

away, into the camouflage of crowds
where all the nights borne by the insane,
conned old con artist will cry out,
and he'll never again take another train.

IN FLOOD

(Áradatban)

> *in my dreams silence has made*
> *an appearance in human shape*
> (J.A.)

Plain and pale I am like peeled tree roots,
like someone whose eyes clearly reflect
the choking seizures of innocent deer and
the vultures that on his throat collect;

tender, too, I am like someone who swings
a shirt and a cooking pot in his neuron net,
fattens frogs inside his lungs and would like
to dry our dreams we haven't dried out yet,

I'm also just the lost son of the algae-
smeared silence in a sunken continent,
who keeps going although he knows:—
they will come for him, too, at the end.

A RING OF LOMBARDY POPLARS

(Jegenyekör)

Under my heart there's a space about
as wide as a hand or three.

This is where the wind herds
and lashes the foliage,
the grassy rushes, the grumbling animals.

The yellow teeth of ruminating oxen
whorl, munch, chatter at the moon,
millions of little creatures,

on their skin pearly whips bubble up.
This is where downpours drum, where lightning strikes,

where whirling wheel hubs turn
and grind to dust my dreams
that hiss like grass.
Like milk, goodness overflows from the valley,
sin burns with alcohol flame.

Why are the Lombardy poplars
standing in a ring
dressed in uniform and
menace?

They cast a shadow of silvery sword swish—
their sway is razor thin.
Like hay kicking between the jaws of oxen,
man lives, fears, flounders
—and rises from the convulsing ground.
Gods tempt him with squash and mulberries!

There's no way out—
the ring of Lombardy poplars is closed!
The wind has no wings!
They live in the depths, those who live,
wound-up, like the clock in the pot.

Under my heart a lightning bolt:
that's what lights a fire here,
there's no other way out except up,
like smoke from under the kettle,
only up!!!
like
s
m
o
k
e

PSALM

(Zsoltár)

Yes, we fell in with the herd again
and you, lord, through our palms raised up toward you,
drive your spikes sent in a shower
and poisoned they are, all your showers,
you come before us in a mist of smoke and sulfur.
Here we stand, nailed down cold,
rearing up on hind legs
still to praise you.
Your waters gush below
the windows of our faces in deep welts,
they keep on gushing
over the suppliant fields of our childhood,
over all its prancing colts,
 its curly lambs,
 its gentle grasses,
 its golden apples.

You promised manhood, yet you wash
our youth from us, but why?
Why visit upon us the tepid stench of
wet dogs and the smell of poverty?
Here we stand,
nailed down cold
by your spikes and
pagan wrath,
still singing your praises
till the food slops slime-like from our lips,
and falls away the water glass.

DON'T TRUST...

(Ne higgy...)

Don't trust the silence
of grass, trees and woods.
    They live in tight
    little stirs,
    if you take a deep breath,
    you sense
    the noise they disperse—

Don't trust the clumsy
silence of plain objects.
    Your forceful movements
    are burning in them—
    and so are your dreams.

Gleam of perspiration falls
    in asphalt,
the traces of hard nails
    in freshly built walls,
in yellow cornfields
    the fever of shiny hoes:

    through them the fidgeting
    of your hand silently shows.

Watch out for objects, handle them,
pack them carefully, even if picayune:
    after you die
    they can still injure the moon—

AGAINST THE HORROR

(Az iszony ellen)

We sure make a sorry picture:
        —plop!—
and terror holds us in its grip.
Yet all that happened was that through
itself the faucet squeezed a drip.

One little squeak—and the house
to the stars is rocketed—by the shock...
In convulsions jumps
the man inside and
bites into the corn-meal crock.

The woman vomits. Clutching her hands
on her stomach, counts the minutes:
one... two... three... six...
Soon the child is also demented
behind the grill of fingertips.

I alone, a kid without
a shirt on my back,
go recruiting a host against the horror—
and mount an attack.

Hey! all ye kisses of the world,
come, come gather here! Carefree hugs and love scenes,
fond caresses, let them be my host!
And you, whose nerves are wound up by machines,
don't let pain cremate your faces
each into a speechless roast!
Hey! the warmth of all the handshakes
stored away over a thousand years!
Don't you people feel it? Couldn't it keep
the solar system spinning on its gears?

But you only stare: what's he yelling about?
On my words inside you horror tramples like a bull.
That's it, I surrender.
It's a lot more powerful.

TOGETHER

(Együtt)

Into a disinfected cloud of b.o.
I, of my free will, let my own body be laid,
somewhat sickened, somewhat of an orphan,
in the middle of a soul-consuming plague.

Maybe it's a sin to watch the sick noise,
air as slurped away from breathless lips,
and the way the skin gets scraped off
by the eager nails before its hour dips,

maybe, it's a sin to chew away the secret
binding life and death where even light is ill;
that's why your suspicions swirl around me
with your heavy breathing, apt to kill,

but while laid up, open to infection,
we're not marked one by one, singly by the pain,
and we'll bounce back so much tougher, for we don't
rock together in the cribs of death in vain.

IN SEEPAGE

(Szivárgásban)

Sitting through a drunken bout, with my prime in sober
                                      sprout,
        at nausea-fed banquets,
I raise my head above the fog,
        my neck as rigid as a log,
in the midst of God's own revelry
that smarts the dreams' corroding hide
and turns the childhood blue inside,
while He drums with rainbow fingers
keeping the beat on skulls and spines.
Sitting through a drunken bout, at nausea-fed banquets,

I report on what my burning red-eyes show me:
    the Wonder of Wonders is seeping
    from us ever so slowly.

Soundlessly off it flies, like a draft in breezy skies,
seeping in unseen plies, like the blood welling up
                among the feathers of an eagle stoned,
trickling off or gushing in any splendid guise,
no mere stone can block its way—and no rhyme intoned;
it swirls all around me,
around my stiffened weighty head
licking salt out of my tears,
dousing dignity in floods of fever,
pilfering my sacred message birds,
leaching out from underneath my tongue
the thousand-year-old cave-lit words,
and eating into sustaining phrases
like an acid with flameless blazes
into steel's bold edge.

Rush to the rescue? Hell, no! Let the seepage prevail!
Forget the plaster for the breach and the cut!
Let the playful trickle cheer up the fracas out there
and let the roadside weeds in green go flaming, but
let life resound! And if our skin dries up

around us like a shell, let's pretend we're well
on our way as a red planet lighting up the skies:
                    a sour berry high up on a branch!
I no longer stand on guard, nor do I compromise!

I'll get down to work here, at the drunken bout,
                    with my prime in sober sprout,
                    where seepage festers, springs a leak.
I'll urge corrosive action words.
I'll inflame the marrow and the veins to shriek,
what steals away from us is renewed at once
in the hands of our dreams and *vigilant organs*,
     we shrink and we grow
     we shrink and we grow
     but we're here! and we go
and join the banquet, let wrinkles give us no support:
     —we're alive! we're breathing! thus
     on the Wonder of Wonders
     again and again I report!

THE OLD SCHOOL:
FARKAS GYMNASIUM

(Farkas utca)

The stone cradle of this land,
the orphaned infant crib
of our century's
orphan spirit.
(It was lined by the fern whispers
of cooling forest streams
for the student that here I was
to rock my growing dreams.)

Mezöség, Szilágy, strong Hunyad,
    and remote
Szeklerland sprouted out of here
like a collar from a coat—
    and I watch here grow
—from seeds cast by a stone hand—
history's grand show.

Ghosts of past greats stand on guard;
    gigantic Bethlen-snowstorms,
      Apáczai's holy fires
        flare up at this crest.
The Old Tower's cold regard
falls on hungry Házsongárd—
where defenders of the first
in peace are laid to rest.

I come by here with sugar cubes
for Sir Saint George's horse
and feed them to him from my hand.
It's high time
to spear that slime
and stop trying to snake-charm
    the newer dragons of the land!

Nurtured is a future, broad
　with patience, fairness taught
　　by the Cradle,
　　and a new grade'll
face the "mene tekel" eyes—
(And it'd only nicely fit
if I were named after it
upon my demise!)

(*Mezőség, Szilágy, Hunyad are regions famous for their old battle grounds; Bethlen and Apáczai were patriotic leaders; Szeklerland is Transylvania, the home of Szeklers, a branch of the Hungarian nation; the Old Tower is part of the original fortifications of Kolozsvár, a major city and cultural center of Transylvania; Házsongárd is a cemetery; this college-preparatory school is named after a 19th century namesake of the poet, Farkas; "mene tekel" is a quote from the Hebrew Bible meaning "has been weighed and found wanting".)*

INTERROGATION

(Vallató)

The hide to the marketplace doesn't come cheap,
there is no fox in it, muskrat askew.
Often I dream about skinning my friends:
Why keep so silent? Yes, you? And you? And you?

THE CHOSEN OF PERFECTION: JÁNOS BOLYAI

(A tökély kiszemeltje)

To make it work with the facts it can reap,
I made my mind a colt with embers to leap,
and myself as its go-for, brash and brave,
I became Perfection's chosen slave.

But I can't surrender to this brute
eternity about to strike me mute,
to a power without the face I seek,
to a tyrant that proves to be too weak,
to empty space that has no sky
for thought—a witness there to testify.

There's my stubborn will it must face—
its sandals are not for me to unlace,
I will not be saddled with a world
unless it's one that I myself unfurled.

Let Perfection reel and madly plough
over me for I've discovered how
from old embers a new flame to nurse—
from Nothingness the next universe!

(János Bolyai, 1809-1860, Transylvanian mathematician, whose non-Euclidean geometry served as a cornerstone to Einstein's theory of relativity. The last line is a quote from a letter he sent to his father.)

THE ROAR OF THE SCOURGESONG

(Ostorzúgásban)

Fooled by Death I am, the grip of
an ancient thirst around me curls,
laughs out loud by Mount Zion
watching how among the swine we
lightly cast our precious pearls.

Another kind we'd rather be,
another word quakes every lip,
another kind of dreams are sinking
with us on the Final Ship.

In the century's wrecked plazas
it stands among the naked wrongs;
lashes roar out its sore secrets and
grimly glowing wild songs.

Chewed up are now all its dreams and
curses sizzle from this thirst;
in our graveyard of messiahs
merry crows are twanging lyres
with the bright eyes of the cursed.

We don't need flutes and strings to ply us,
desires' dance with us to flip;
just give us Ady Endre's whip,
just give us Ady Endre's whip!

*(In order to preserve the aural as well as visual impact of a name it is
sometimes presented in its original Hungarian form with the surname
first, followed by the given name. This is the case here with Ady Endre, a
poet from the turn of the century who had been influenced by the French
symbolist school and, in turn, had a great influence on subsequent gen-
erations of Hungarian poets. His brand of patriotism was coupled with
social criticism resulting in a "tough love" attitude toward his country;
hence, the metaphorical "whip".)*

TO SÁNDOR KÁNYÁDI

(Kányádi Sándornak)

On the rivers of Nyikó, Küküllö, Maros and Olt
they climb into dough-kneading tubs,
or into old wash-basins,
the children,
and one of them is sure to make it to the Ocean.

In our territorial waters when a ship goes down
the rats are the first
to dive off the deck.

Never were we gung-ho lads
or even second lieutenants,
and surely no respected captains.
But we can pass for modest fiddlers
of simple shepherd tunes,
on a teeny flute
with laboring throats
and lips turning blue
in spastic desperation
we keep on playing, don't we, Brother,
to the final seconds
just the way that band did
on the deck
of the Titanic.

(Sándor Kányádi, 1929-, Hungarian poet, also born in Transylvania.)

OUR RESERVES

(Tartalékaink)

We rake over the old ash pile and bake
apples on the remaining embers and a squash.
We bury potatoes in the root cellar, in softly
sniffling sand the carrots, we put out the bubbling
craters of the prune preserve, send out for extra
canning jars; rattling above us is a wax paper sky.
We finish up this year's lard spreading it on bread
for the children, on their feet we pull up
flannel socks, explaining that winter's on its way.
Winter's on the way.

TAVERN SMOKE

(Kocsmafüst)

The handle of the ax that's struck into the door post is still ashake,
and like mute stumps, the lumberjacks are sitting in brandy haze;
what begins in here its whistling,
with its icy slivers sizzling,
is a mountainous gale.

It races through the room, the clouds of smoke,
and suddenly old words,
long buried in the sour cellars of the tongue,
catch on fire and so do hopes, aged into faces,
and demands deposited on teeth;
next the fire leaps onto the rancid haystacks
        —so much like here the hair packs—
of troubles—finally!
The faces slowly char to black, the sizzling stench
of burning flesh engulfs the place:
        —a crematory of candor this is.
Sticking out are leg bones.

Outside it's a crow-winged night and silence.

Only in God's own barnyard is there howling: the hounds.
Hunkered down and backed into a corner they watch
as the ax stuck in the door post, with frightening slowness,
begins to melt.

COLD SPELL

(Hideg)

Vitriol blue floods the sky,
whitewashed is the War-Path Milky Way,
silver snow and dust-fine snow
somehow keep the dirt at bay.

Strawberry vines cry in the snow
—the hidden nerves of winter freeze—
from the Carpathian Mountains
hermits fly in with the breeze.

I keep on stoking my make-believe
no-camp-fire for the flock,
better if they stand around
a thing to fear and not to mock.

I keep on stoking and the War God
yawns out loud, he's half asleep,
but should I ever close my eyes
He'd sick on us the dogs of sleet.

*(In Hungarian mythology the Milky Way is regarded as the War Path of
the ancestors riding to the rescue.)*

EARLY SPRING

(Kora tavasz)

The snow will get a shock and reel off the mountains,
                                          won't it,
and the white-wrapped, puffing ruins of existence will be
revealed; the snow will slide off the land, and a forsaken
autumn dream, rusting to a tree leaf, will pulsate
uncovered, and its trash piles sleeping under the snow—
hip-hop—will then disappear, won't they? And when
this winter-world starts shedding its skin, shaking off
the pure white gauze of freeze, surely its true face will
bust out, when stubborn-seed skulls break out with slow
ground-bark freeze; and when the snow-fur trim slips
off the branches, will a rich burden raise its bud-skull up,
up!, and up!, will the mistletoe-laden limb rise, too?
While grass and new wheat: the soil's green wells up
into sunshine, it will not be choked by the foam of melting
snow, will it? Hard winters are followed by wild springs,
summers and stern autumns,
but manpower also heats this earth, its seasons
chattering from snow and glow,
and the freeze will release from its hand
the throat of the song birds
stuck here with it, won't it?

IN SERVITUDE

(Szolgálatban)

You twisted my arms off and planted them in Elysian Fields, you're
roasting venison slices, hugging gypsy girls in its shade, and red wine
gushes from the corners of your mouth as you watch it with roars of
laughter: whispering foliage of my hand over you shows the middle
finger.
My legs do not bend at the knees, and you buried them up to the knees.
The earth pours out its produce with great humility, I can't very well
sneak off either—look, they smashed two flies with one swat.
Your well-groomed sons stretched my eardrums on drums.
Even Bartok's corpse, kicked blue already, also jerks when whacked.
My commandeered services go stuttering around you;
from my strands of hair, turning white one by one, I might weave
a reed silk bunch
for hunting hats.
But please forgive me:
I cannot
control
my gaze
either.
It radiates to meadows, awakening, and rousting sleepers,
it admonishes my arms: back where you belong!
To hug, to kill, to brawl—
that's your business.
It digs me out of the ground: always keep going toward a steeple,
it says, and my eardrum falls in with the rhythm of the heartbeat.
I'm afraid, you take this as rebellion on my part.
And yet, it is while in service that death catches up with me,
my skin's dampness turns into steel.

THE QUARRY MINER POET

(Kőgörgető)

Hello up there, in silicate glow!
when the jeering laughter from below dies out,
and the adoring looks fall off in rags
from the skin of Saint Uselessness,
abandoned by the wrath of the Gods,
man will be left alone with the Stone.
Nothing else but the caustic of sweat,
and only blood seeping from his hands and shoulders,
only knives of murderous pain
in the flesh, sinews,
only the fainting—
But then the hero of legends looks to the side,
and there: on the precipices of millennia
many a versifier: Quarry miner!
raising his voice, rage, laughter, curses,
the fate of the ill-fated into the Sun—
Let the arms just relax—and the cliff crumbles!
Let the knees buckle—and you're buried!
Go on then, on and on! Until you bust your gut!
Even if it seems from below:
the poets are gently floating,
hanging on to stone balloons
they're flying heaven-bound—

ARCHEOLOGY

(Régészet)

Stop this playing with our skeletons!
Squandered they are passed from hand to hand.
Wasted did we spend those ages
scouring the graves of Szeklerland?

Look at this, a real backbone, look how
glowingly it reaches for the sun.
Look at this great gleaning-cleaning job
all these busy little worms have done!

Elbows you collect without the flesh,
and cheekbones, too, without the searing eyes—
there's a great demand for skulls on desks
for a something there to—symbolize!

Look, how skeletons now rally!
I shall dress them up in steel and flesh,
we shall plow the fallow lands—the skulls
then will possess their ancient force afresh.

Stop this playing with our skeletons,
squandered they are passed from hand to hand.
Digging for them then I'll have to go
to the graves of old Assyrian land...

THE SMELL OF SNOW

(A hó szaga)

The white shadows of my fingers glide over the terrain—:
leaves of grass vitrify; the beet picker blows under his
nails.
Dogs are coughing in a distant doghouse,
a jay flock sounds off here and there.
Steaming herds are swallowing the fog of fall with
whistling lungs, the smell of manure is thickening, giving
off heat.
Faces brimming with patience are watching
the swaying-swinging five-pointed moonlight,
and suddenly
a handbreadth's
light ignites on a distant peak,
a raw breeze rises—
and with wide open nostrils, jostling,
they all rear up, all, all, and
up————
from where the smell of danger
and purity delivers a whack here—
the SNOW!

GENTLE TUNE

(Dúdoló)

A snowfall I'd like to be, blessing all,
landing on every crumpled face on earth,
a consoling-big, sonorous song,
the breath of the great universe.

A snowfall I'd like to be, as if in
the mood and the cash to shop for snow,
enough for a man of measly skin
to have snowfall all year long to go.

Slowly like someone unrequested,
I'd hover over earth as a song,
in a single shirt I'd rock it gently,
and my passing I would not prolong.

I'd be the short shirt of the universe;
I'd choose my garments for plain poverty,
to keep freezing dreams and shivering
souls late at night from pounding me.

A snowfall I'd like to be, blessing all,
landing on every crumpled face on earth,
reassuring to even those in fever.
Graceful in death as well as in birth.

TUNNELS IN THE SNOW

(Alagutak a hóban)

Did I want to sift like snow?
        Look at that blizzard fall!
Over my homeland wild flakes are
        whipping up a squall.
Up to the knees, the waist, the throat,
        grow the choking piles,
        white foam builds up in lewd globs
        on the steeple-spires.

Now the snow sits sky-high over us!

Quiet and without a budge
in the Great Swaddling life is
learning to be still at home,
the edges of scythes and sickles are
swaddled up to the sky's dome.
The strangled wheezing of the villages is
white and whiter it's to grow,
no stone clangs against another,
lips are bursting not with words but snow—
in the belly of snow mounds the intellect
peacefully sits back to rest.

      Let's dig tunnels in the snow!

Roads by the thousands, each one groping for its mate!
here the pulse can melt the snow
    and dreams can circulate
    in the unclogged veins
    of simple joys and pains!
The heartbeat of towns and villages resounds,
the heavy white of winter thickened lies;
prudent passion, doubting faith,
let them operate the laser beams of our gaze
      searching for
        each other's eyes!

Let's dig tunnels in the snow!

Steady intent, sudden moves,
brittle dreams, the shivering mind,
must not live forever
with the flesh of snow entwined.

But when ejected by our mouths
        at last this celestial cotton falls
and the music's not by frozen bands,
let the feet rejoice then in a stomping dance,
and around us
let the Hymn melt world-sized halls!

DÓZSA-FACE

(Dózsa-arc)

I've got neither peace nor sin,
it's a grave shirt I'm crackling in;
but they're breaking just my body—:
breaking me down to purity.
Like dogs at the burning Moon:
they're jumping on my throat, my doom,
gnawing me with wrathful barks.
I smile even if their howl smarts;
I watch with saint superiority
as they beautifully devour me.

György Dózsa (1470—20 July 1514) was a soldier from Transylvania who led a peasants' revolt against the kingdom's landed nobility. He was eventually defeated, tortured, and executed along with his followers.

THE LAST MINING HORSE

(Az utolsó bányaló)

Two thousand years in shafts of time,
around and around,
or tied to the manger of Nazareth,
I've had enough.

My eyes have fossilized already,
carbonized in the choking blackness,
the signals of swaying lamps, fake lights
and fake truths have dropped off into whirling depths.
I keep bumping into the black wall of nothing
in this compulsive, stubborn walking in place.
You don't have to tremble when I suddenly raise my head,
I'm not rebelling yet,
only listening to the billion-year-old grass buzz
and foliage whisper roaring around me;
oh, because what sonorous,
what delicious treasures of
the world are turning to dust here.

Only now that the soggy glow of the sweat
collected on my chest starts shining through the skin
and broiling brightness lights up all regions
inside me,

the blood in my arteries is frothing up,

my mane is stiffening up,

my hooves are turning rock hard,

they rumble and break through the wall of the damp night—
and the light, the light, the forever promised, forever hidden
earthly light whose bombs beautified my body that's now
exploding, my flesh comes apart, into pink rags...
EAT THEM!

THE LAW

(Törvény)

To totally shrink, to become totally tiny
from the pain and hide in the pod of green
sweet peas, and then, with hands clutched behind,
to walk up and down in its halls colored by the coolness
of plant life, between walls pulsing with green veins,
just to wait,
to wait until this settles down, this magnificent and
awe-inspiring creation of the world that for the past
million years has been rampaging and testing our nerves...
             ...it's no use—
it's no use, because with spectral fidgeting
the vitreous peas start swelling in order to
conquer their empire therein; alarmed and
in despair, your breath burst open the green
coffin that's rapidly filling up with alien life—

and you'll have to stand up straight again
and face the light wielding a sparkling knife—

EVENING FEVERS

(Esti lázak)

And they will come for you, the evening fevers,
inside your skin needles play music,
on the balcony Chagall's tunes
play off and on,
everything that leaves footprints
in the evening: singing, singing, singing.

Songs over the a snow field
where a herd of wolves is galloping,
and no traces of rabbit tracks
or deer tracks are to be found
they encircle solitary
wild pear trees,
tufts of their fur on the bark
goes on singing;
the wolf-hair strings on the wild pear tree bark
resonate with the wind in the woods,
hearing it the lamb brays trembling,
here inside, in a cradle of books.

And already splotches of sounds,
colors, wild roses, out in the snow,
your wild roses drowning
in snow-Sahara, go slow
with your silent fear, look, the herd,
the wild beasts are already too far to see,
from the corner of my eye
sorrowful death is drinking their pee.
The evening fevers will come for you,
roses of blood grow in the snow.
Still young, with a holiday song by Chagall,
you'll soon blend into the fever's glow.

Dec 22, 1989

LATHER

(Tajték)

To László Tökés

Axes have driven this pine up the mountain,
it trudges gasping up and up
while axes roared behind for years.
Almost reached the peak: the whiteness
you see on its branches is not snow—:
lather, that's what it is,
rising suds!

Dec 22, 1989

BLACK CHRISTMAS

(Fekete Karácsony)

Should snow fall now, it would run off the face
of the earth, so overheated are the hearts around here.
Innocent glances scamper up to the sky: "Has Jesus
been born yet? Is that really possible?"
Priests in our churches, poets under a fractured sky, both
are trying to fool any humility-prone heart,
but no such thing can be found.
The white heat of last year's bloody Christmas washed off
with the melting snow of March, got soaked up
by the heat of June,
and here we are again, waist deep in advent,
bamboozled folks with empty hands: "If you should
come, my Lord, I'll stand before you."
And the Lord is not to be seen in any shape or form.
Double-crossed, crushed into poverty, the soul is
still trying to jump above the waves, but, defrauded of
its jewels, it falls asleep on the banks of its mere
existence.
Until it shakes itself awake.
And then only the piety of Christmas can dampen the soul's
whipped-up rage for a few hesitant minutes,
while it gently, almost apologetically,
strokes the cheeks of loved ones
with a hand buzzing of emptiness:
"I worked hard, I struggled for this love, but that's all
that's left of it," the hand jerks into a fist, and an angel
with blown-up feet flies off with the remaining hope.
In its cold place there are only children,
unsuspecting little children asking questions:
"My Lord, what will we have to eat tomorrow?"
A black Christmas has come upon us, we're
floundering on its broken angel wings,
we're tearing at its kidneys and liver:
"We'll have ourselves to devour, my son!"

WILD DILL

(Vadkapor)

My friends, you've stolen the woods;
the Vienna Woods of operettas would sing to you
if you cared to stick your money-scented noses
in its direction. Up here in the Carpathians a few oxen oaks
remain, their north side covered with flat mushrooms.
But I don't care to have them without you.
I'm thinning down like a wild grapevine winding
its way through bundles of barbed-wire fences
plundered from borders. I'm losing weight, losing it
to the dwindling evening lamplight,
for the lack of near or far friends
I vegetate; this way, and only this,
from between claws.
But if you should ever see
a wild dill bloom
in the glorious Kärntner Strasse, don't
put it in a vase. It is a parachute,
from my land.
Only man can escape this way
in aerial space from regions
where everything is in the midst of breaking,
where hearts, gizzards, livers are chiseled,
and it's not crying but only wild dill that can help
with its parachute to land in cool Europe's
hottest plaza, where at least there's music,
the music of folks dreamed free,
sung liberated.
This is where I'm going to touch down, armed
with blue-wildflower-submachineguns, dandelion bayonets,
and by a parachute which is: a wildflower.
Don't worry, I'll be passing through,
a fly-by guest, a mendicant on the fly
against the nonexistence of the West,
a freelance parachutist,
a tame wild dill.

AT THE EDGE OF PERMANENT SNOW

(Az örök hó határán)

> *"...Because Árpád Farkas speaks like this*
> *I expect no mercy, no favors at all!*
> *I stuff the barrel of a gun with this verse*
> *And splash my brain cells on the wall."*
> *(László Vári Fábián: Of this Earth)*

A gun barrel stuffed with poems stays mute,
you can choke it with flowers, it will not shoot;
you can't set off a flower-verse revolution
with the levers of a heart in flight, pursued.

You must break the gun in half on your knee,
and you'll be holding a steel and a wooden club,
that's how we kill each other the good old way
with the help of the Balkan orangutan hub.

The wild beasts of these new times are coming
to the wake, and the reckless weeds of the terrain
scurry down your throat—cries out the song
that remains with you—and I, too, remain

at the edge of permanent snow, here. Then: higher!
Like someone to whom God will not throw
a thing to eat and whose diet is Sahara's sand,
I devour sovereign borders—: untamed snow

is what I digest—far horizons! Paralyzed
angels can get to heaven chewing on this fare,
unarmed but always higher, where a peak shines—,
ever higher, even if there's nothing up there.

BLOOD-SOAKED SNOW

(Véres Havak)

I gobbled snow last night, nearly choked on it,
blood-soaked snow. You said it would color
the whines breaking out of my throat;
this here is the Danube's ice, still lacking reflection,
only its color is that of wild strawberries, and there,
the one swimming without a head, pistachio.
You didn't invite me to this kind of five-o'clock tea, my sluttish
Madonna, nor to find Southern Europe
in this kind of a wash basin. This here is a Serbian leg,
there a Croatian arm, Hungarian
eyeball. This is not the kind of peace we dreamed
the summer of seventy-one in Csurgo
when we were trumpeting blood-red water melon
between our teeth, we of strange names, so many of us,
not this kind of Danube Basin,
with Palics Lake conked out, fish soup of Eszek with
lots of blood-red mushrooms, there, where
there was still room, "where it's okay for you to read".
Only ruins are left of poems and cities: carrion stench!
Glorious members of the avant garde! Your time has arrived!
The tongue, as a stew ingredient is ripped out
already. No need to chew over the question of
"modern" human speech!
Machineguns stutter your songs.
Only the poor, whether they be peasants,
poets, actors unable to turn mute, know
how they're going to be interred, according to what rite
 if they fall flat on the back now.
Feverishly, with the greatest humility,
I swallow the blood-soaked snow, one or two bone splinter
cuts open my throat, but that's not what I choke on.
We wanted the West, in a New Byzantium? Here, take it,
fresh snow, knife-fork-submachinegun all laid out,
have a fancy breakfast under the sky of this insolently
corrupt and treacherous, wide and beautiful Europe!

THE SONG OF A SELF-MADE BIRD

(Jómadárdal)

Someone flies over me,
a birdman perhaps, wings swinging,
it is now that we're losing someone
never to replace him with another,
new, self-made bird.
I rise to tiptoes to catch his sight:
his size is that of a skull;
he could pass though this narrow chasm
to see: how skulls can fly off on the wings
of overgrown ears.
Let his triumphant flight lash,
from potato nest nauseous great intellect
skipping from one skull to the next,
dense defiance—
while baby dreams are whining
under twig blankets.
The curse of "greatness" demands the sky.
Our indolence is your bowl.
And in the bowl proud men
who know exactly where
the fish lay their roes…
will you lay roes somewhere?
I know the beastly big nothingness
makes no note of our existence
neither does it acknowledge:
our skulls belong to us.
Myriads of tiny moths from the dead,
and the able-bodied can hardly breathe.
Is this possibly a gap that would allow
Almightiness to pass through Transylvania?
If it isn't, it isn't. But it's no matter
of indifference what people eat around me
from my claws. I thought
if we revolted at least my daughter might
achieve salvation in a school of achitecture
in Kolozsvár and will light candles for the dead:
it makes no sense to build here anymore,

so get right to it! You old dogs.
To listen to your yelps,
he'll stay around,
only his lovely mane and skull
will wing far off
with the fading light signals
from your city of sties

IN WHETSTONE WEATHER

(Köszörű-időben)

So the fever finally got you in this whetstone weather!
Rain gutters rattle diamond teeth overhead,
 snow lights up my bones, the snow flakes
on my skin turn to beads of sweat.

The word is dancing in my rosy throat,
 it jumps up and down like the thermometer,
it'd change its mind hundreds of times,
but eventually it blisters out....
     yelping though,
whining like a vinyl winter coat.

And it zooms towards you, boys, in its way
phlegm-fogged winds are splitting the air,
false traditions, wrinkle-size chains
preparing to tie you up.
Leave the damp socks, the alarmed question
marks alone at night if they swing lazily
          hung on wires bare—,
and if you get drunk on your first pay check—after
such a long fast—I don't care.

The compass in your fingers dreams up a sun,
snaps, and slaps you on your shoulder
with a wild universal gust.
The gaping mouth of the vise can crack the
knuckles of your fingers by exhaling musky dust.

A ghost in a pure white coat is roaming the night,
from his hand pills—: doves soar
into the sky.
You dwarfish docs, you'll freeze before
then to cracklings, but it's your blood for which
the aflicted of Europe cry!

There remains the fever, doesn't it, boys,
lily-flamed noise blaring in our veins.

The spine stretches up to the sky, doesn't it, but
it cannot wind around a rainbow! There remains
faith, doesn't it, the all defeating light,
and we will not hide out like aged beasts,
slobbering and licking the open wounds of our fight.

THE RISK

(Kockázat)

While somewhere the gods
were sleeping in deep Atlantic silence
I felt like playing a game
and had the tiger taught compliance.

I played ball with Earth
on the sofa—I open my eyes and ears:
should the wilderness now resound—,
it'd cost me a thousand years.

THE SEWER

(A csatorna)

Get going, get deformed, if you must follow the sewer to
the end;
get thinner and thicker, design the dimensions of your
body to fit in,
don't look forward, it's no use, the light of the exit does
not flash,
thin down to a thread, get refined and absorbed in peace,
it's no use, no one's waiting for you at the end.

A HAND WAVE

(Integető)

Through the steam
of the tea kettle
from the armpits of distant
mountains the foggy outlines
of dear folks emerge,
so many kind faces pulsate
the tender Morse signals
of heartbeats:
you're not alone, don't worry,
the ties of brother-care is our gift
until the fog begins to lift.

LINDEN LEAF

(Hársfalevél)

A raindrop on a linden leaf—:
How young yet: a pearl built with trepidation over
a hundred years: vibrating from the deep as if
the eternal sun and the evening star of long-ago summers
were shining through its rain-sloshed skin,
the low hanging branches of misty forest alleys
were simmering in it, north-country and Transylvanian
wagons trudging, mountains, rivers, villages, roads:
pulsating temple arteries or the disarrayed
hair strands of unfaithful women,
and the waving of endlessly stretched-out farewell songs—:
all that has disappeared now shines from
a raindrop trembling on a linden leaf:
or is it a pearl already? Has it been slapped
into a demented diamond-globe by whacking time?
A pair of night-brown eyes
are glowing in its sparkling center,
and they watch you, just watch you folks.

WHERE RAIN AND SNOW MEET

(Hol az eső összeér a havazással)

In this monotonous rain I'm begging,
how many thousands of years have I been trudging
in your tracks?
My words have filled the ground with panicky
animals so as to allay your fears,
also with shivering woods so as to warm you up;
far behind us,
in the abandoned openings of concepts
now the grass resounds green in vain—
Oh, how many thousands of years have we been trudging
in this monotonous sobbing,
under the eyelashes of the night?
Look, you bend aside the strands of rain
in front of you;
their edges, their coldness snap back at me.
What kind of a march is this,
what kind of magic,
that prevents me from cutting my own trail
before we reach that era
when the rain meets snow,
and my dream continents swim away
in milk-white mist;
covering them white
with snow
I too will fall asleep
forever—

FOR HIS MOTHER'S LOST HAIR

(Anyja elhullott hajára)

The rays were meant to cure you but instead
they bombed the hair off your head,
cut down your dense ornament,
my childhood refuge was its tent,
a forest in a secret land,
alive to touch, strand by strand,
and yet a screen against all threats,
all troubles and upsets;
I took shelter in its locks
when I had to flee
the thundering sky
and its uglier glee.......
....
Mother, don't you cry for your hair, let brushes weep,
Toss the loyal combs, expensive shampoos into a heap,
don't you cry, mother, don't cry for your mane,
the most beautiful of all the women you still remain:
it's for your life the silky whisper of the field is sent,
and I'll weave a halo for your head's ornament.

WHEN HOPE SPRINGS FROM GRAVES

(Ha sírokon hajt ki a remény)

I'm standing on Cemetery Hill: my last grandparent is the dead.
Around me a small crowd: every beathing soul of a small hamlet
consisting of less than forty cottages;
every weather-beaten face is crowding here in their Sunday best,
because a confederate in the century-old problem has joined them:
on a rumbling casket machine
the 88-year old Aunt Erzsi is here;
in her ten-year absence weeds have slowly overrun
the courtyards of her mind and house in vain;
she's finally found her way back to her tiny village by the Nyikó River,
in the aging, wrinkled heart of Székelyszentmiklós,
a place that by the end of the century had sent ten times
as many children into the world than its present population,
rolling them far away, so that even the living have a hard time
finding their way home let alone the dead; she too is awaited by
absolution in the form of a flower swaying between her clutching
fingers, because the house of shared memories is awakened
from summers of working together, the rattle of thrashing,
the hissing Stalinist years and from the carefree May festivals
the blinking heat and shine of community spirit splashes up; and look:
every man of the village, all twelve of them between the ages of
fifty and seventy (modern-day KömívesKelemen?)
are digging the grave for the widow of János Farkas,
nee Erzsébet Kibédi with muscle-tearing effort,
as if each of them were digging his own,
as if they believed:
the land of communal spirit
will become eternal from their crumbling bodies.

I'm standing on Cemetery Hill, the wind rummages in my hair
with its long fingers, nagging me: what could be scampering
in the mind of this forty-year old man who's burying his
last grandparent
now at the edge of a new chasm of a man's life;
this wind gets hold of a microphone-twig equipped to detect
thoughts behind thoughts and overhear even soundless cordial voices
and bends it toward my lips:

how have you, my good man, comported yourself
under the silver showers of the last four decades, how have you
managed to avoid St. Michael's horse with skin unscathed,
whereas your hallowed predecessors already at the age of twenty six
and thirty two
pulled the marble blocks of their lifetime achievement
down on themselves;
did it make any sense, and what sense could it have made
that escaping the more forgiving grip of
providence
you lit up your nights with the lightning bolts of paper sheets,
and humming newfangled shaman chants you plundered
sunken cemeteries,
begging your ancestors' bones from the ground with a laser gaze,
and the ground keeps shaking and trembling,
like a sponge it keeps soaking in crowds of the living;
what was the use of the March and July songs
if summer was always followed by fall,
and winter by May snow showers;
what was the use of your entreats to the Snow,
the parable demanding a companion in the frostbitten
existence stuffed with snow,
if by the age of forty you are abandoned by the living,
by friends;
one after another the girls with flashing white ankles,
fleeting friends crawl into the dirt or the distant mist...
and the herding, the gallop, whips cracking on the skin
of belligerent beasts,
reeling into singing, stuttering into verse—what were they good for?

I'm standing on Cemetery Hill, talking to twigs
eavesdropping with tiny leaves for ears; I speak into the wind:
your prying questions, please stop hurting me!—:
I wasn't really a poet, I was simply full of fears.
I graciously lived through these forty years of dread,
and since I, too, was born a wrinkled, bawling
and shivering babe,
they covered me with fuzzy lullabies,
and I already panicked: let the warming song never cease;
I build barns out of noodles, forts out of sand;
let it never get overgrown!— holding my breath I hummed
magic incantations; I was in love with a thin-boned,

teeny girl: "Zsuzsanna, please, fall in love with me!"—
mumbling I trembled for her;
I climbed the highland pass of Nagyszoros,
on its top, up on Cemetery Hill, the Sun was aglow,
and the mud jerked me back,
and the snow sucked me inside!
—with hoist-it-now!, cursing-entreating words,
shivering, I kept crawling toward the light;
and nights started coming, my rooms getting stronger,
cracking of branches, wild growls moved into my furniture,
and the beasts of the jungle mooed from the hoarse faucets;
I feared the floating, fleet butterflies,
the body of the nights falling on my shoulders,
and I placed a sheet of paper before me: an oil lamp!;
and the world widened, the earth and the sky before me grew larger,
from the heart of Transylvania I could see distant seas
and planets,
and that the Sun would never rise again: I was in a panic over it;
I filled my skin inside with shiny treasures,
it turned to bronze!, and if knives marching against me tinkled,
I also feared that their edges might get chipped;
I trembled for meadows: while asleep they may be abandoned by dew,
also the oak: in its dream it might tip over;
without me things would not notice
if miracles happened to them;
I worried about the landscape brimming with soul:
if it had secrets, it should not speak in dreams!
if a single blade of grass were to get going, it would
take with it my mother's only smile, like my grandparents
have swum away with the flood of rippling meadows
and surging farmlands,
and now graves are the only buoys—
and so as not to let vinegary ants turn my tongue mute
with their buzz
un-mourned crimson throat,
with my wounded lips I softly sang chunky, berry-size words,
green-leafed incantations, with a hammering heart,
like someone would whistle at night among graves;

but being a poet was far from me, no poet was I;
only fear of the horror made me sing,
with the sweat-faith of twelve grave diggers,

with the wild hope of communal persistence
standing here on Cemetery Hill,
roaring in the face of the wind:
fear we must but bravely! And live. Live.

*(Kömíves Kelemen is a builder in a folktale who is cursed to use
his wife's body in the mortar in order to keep a wall from falling
down.)*

SONG

(Ének)

Life has got to go on, dear.
The shirt is flitting on the line.
The air is crackling all around us:
And our kids are doing fine.

They will write our song tomorrow;
The shirt will turn hard on the line
With its arms up in the wind—
In a time of floods in words
I became here as destined
One of the typewriter nerds.

Life has got to go on, dear,
The shirt's caught in the windy whine.
The air is crackling all around us:
And our kids are doing fine.

THE WANDERER

(Vándor)

One day for sure I, too, will go away,
with old age perhaps, if cancer, a stroke,
a merciful cirrhosis of the liver or something else
fails to come for me sooner—go into this thick cloud,
this linden wilderness that watches my steps.

I'll go barefoot—something I'm warned against:
the road across the centuries is burning hot;
I'll toss my worn-out boots over my shoulders,
roadside dogs will keep grabbing hold of my stick,
I'm lucky if they leave my shins to me;
for shadows my enemies will keep me company.

I was who I was: someone from nowhere,
obstinate and proud kind who fed
robins and eagles of the cliffs from his hand,
who waded into Nothing without a care
although his heart was beating in his boots.

Of course, we cannot set out without footwear;
even though we don't go very far—there will soon
rise from it a flock of jays that will head for home
while I dry my boot rags under the Moon.

But I will forsake neither my faith nor my folks:
on a footloose star the size of a hobnail
I'll start a campfire, and look, my descendants
will wink up at the light that'll prevail.

BIOGRAPHIES

Árpád Farkas, a leading figure in contemporary Hungarian literature, a poet, translator and journalist, was born in 1944 in Transylvania, Romania, in a Hungarian (also known as *Szekler,*) village where his ancestors had farmed until his father left the land to become a teacher. The postwar years and decades were hard on the family under double oppression, first as members of the Hungarian minority and then as smallholder farmers. His father lost his job and had to do factory work not only to support the family but to pay the exorbitant produce taxes for the grandfather's farm. While attending Babeş-Bolyai University (1961—1966) the future poet already started publishing in periodicals, and in 1967 his work was included in an anthology *Vitorla-ének* (Sail-Song). In 1968 he married a classmate and began his career as a journalist for various publications in various positions, ending up as editor-in-chief at his retirement in 2010. His first poetry volume *Másnapos ének* (Hangover Song) came out in 1968 and was followed by numerous others, including several books of translations, most notably one in 1985 featuring works by Ana Blandiana, a Romanian poet who was blacklisted at the time by the communist regime in spite of her being the president of International PEN. He has been awarded a great number of literary prizes both in Romania and Hungary, most significantly the membership in the Hungarian Academy of Arts, but he is still living in Transylvania, in Sepsziszentgyörgy, a small town with great Hungarian cultural tradition. In his poetry he often speaks out for the survival of his ethnic Hungarian minority in Romania; *Maradok—I Remain*, an anthology of Transylvanian-Hungarian poets, took its title from one of his poems.

Anthologies containing works in translation:
Cântec de fluier, Paul Drumaru, Kriterion, Bucharest, 1972, (in Romanian)
Neue Siebenbürgisch-Ungarische Lyrik, 1974, (German)
Maradok—I Remain, Pro-Print, Romania, 1997
In Quest of the Miracle Stag, Atlantic Centaur Press, Chicago, 2003

The Poetry of Hungary, Ádám Makkai, Chicago, 2003
Dozemii, Sophia, Bulgaria, 1999

Paul Sohar drifted as a student refugee from Hungary to the U.S. where he got a BA degree in philosophy and a day job in chemistry. He took up writing in his adopted language and publishing in every genre, including seventeen volumes of translations, among the latest being *In Contemporary Tense*, poems by Sándor Kányádi (Iniquity Press, 2013) and *Silver Pirouettes*, György Faludy's poetry (Ragged Sky Press, Princeton, 2017). His own poetry: *Homing Poems* (Iniquity Press, 2006) and *The Wayward Orchard*, a Wordrunner Press Prize winner (2011). Other awards: first prize in the 2012 Lincoln Poets Society contest and a second prize from Rode Island Writers Circle prose contest (2014). Translation prizes: the Irodalmi Jelen Translation Prize (2014), Tóth Árpád Translation Prize and the Janus Pannonius Lifetime Achievement Award (both in 2016, Budapest, Hungary). Magazine credits include *Agni*, *Gargoyle*, *Kenyon Review*, *Rattle*, *Poetry Salzburg Review*, *Seneca Review*, etc.

ACKNOWLEDGEMENTS

Grateful acknowledgement is due to the editors of the following publications where some of the poems of this selection were first brought to the reading public:

Anthologies:
Maradok—I Remain, Pro-Print, Romania (1997)
Down Fell the Statue of Goliath, Hungarian Academy of Arts, Budapest (2017)

Literary Journals:
Antinarrative Journal, Blue Unicorn, Loch Raven Review, Ragazine, The Literary Review, To Topos, (US); Peer Poetry Review (UK)

CPSIA information can be obtained
at www.ICGtesting.com
Printed in the USA
FFHW020818171118
49384742-53685FF